MATT MAHER

THE ADVENT OF CHRISTMAS

Illustrated by Mercè Tous

WELLSPRING

North Palm Beach, Florida

THE ADVENT OF CHRISTMAS

ISBN: 978-1-63582-051-5 (hardcover)

Illustrations by Mercè Tous
Art Direction and Design by Ashley Wirfel

Library of Congress Control Number: 2018949277

10   9   8   7   6   5   4   3

Printed in the United States of America

FIRST EDITION

There was a period of several months when my youngest son's bedroom had these weird bulbs in the light sockets. When we'd turn them on, they would flicker; then it always took a few minutes for them to become fully illuminated.

For hundreds of years, Christians have used the four weeks before Christmas as a time to simplify, prepare, and remember the long wait for God's promises in the Old Testament to be fulfilled. As the celebration of Jesus' birth approached, they would also think about Christ's second coming, and with it, they would pray and await the reconciliation of all things. This is the season of Advent.

Advent is a word that comes from the old Latin word *adventus*, which means "arrival." It is a time of year when, as the days grow darker, the light shines brighter. *The Advent of Christmas*—"The Arrival of Christmas"—is a book about these two arrivals, and the way we receive them not as singular events, but as a journey.

As parents with three children, my wife and I are always looking for ways to help our children in their "spiritual seeing." Stories are one of the foundational ways the Church passes on morals, lessons, dreams, and ideals. These stories and narratives are always unfolding and being written in our lives. In an effort to pass the faith on to my children, I wrote a bedtime story about Advent, in the hope that as we read it together every night, the lights will flicker on and begin to illuminate.

It is my hope that this book will provide you and your kids a variety of connection points to the Advent season as well. I pray that as you read through it and the weeks progress, you'll have something to share with your children—and that when Christmas comes, it won't mark the end of a season, but rather the beginning of a wonderful celebration.

—Matt Maher

All is merry and all is bright;
It's the most wonderful time of the year.

Four weeks to slow down in the hustle and bustle,
The Advent of Christmas is here!

To mark the passing of the time,
A wreath of evergreen.
Its leaves show us God's infinite Love,
What Christmas really means.

Upon the wreath five candles sit:
Three purple, one pink, and one white.
The purple for fasting, the pink for rejoicing,
The white for a long Christmas night.

First Sunday! First Sunday! Is it Christmas already?
Hold on! There's four weeks yet to come!

December

01	02	03	04	05	06
07	08	09	10	11	12	13
14	15	16	17	18	19	20
21	22	23	24	25	26	27
29	30	31

More than Santa and presents, we're waiting for Jesus,
With hope for everyone.

We light the second candle for peace
And remember the prophets of old.
Filled with God's glory they start up our story,
"Prepare the way of the Lord!"

This third joyful Sunday is pink for a party!
Gaudete's a word for "rejoice"!
Do not be afraid; his love is strong.
Lift up your heart and your voice!

The fourth week we hear of God's love for all
In the favor and promise to be,
When Gabriel spoke and Mary declared,
"Let it be done unto me."

Four weeks have passed; now a white candle shines
As bright as an evening star
To lead the way for three wise kings
Who traveled from afar.

And this is what all of the waiting is for:
To lead us where Christmas begins—
A tale of a family in Bethlehem,
With no room at the inn.

Joseph and Mary had made their way there
While she had a baby inside.
They had no place to lay their heads,
No home for their special child.

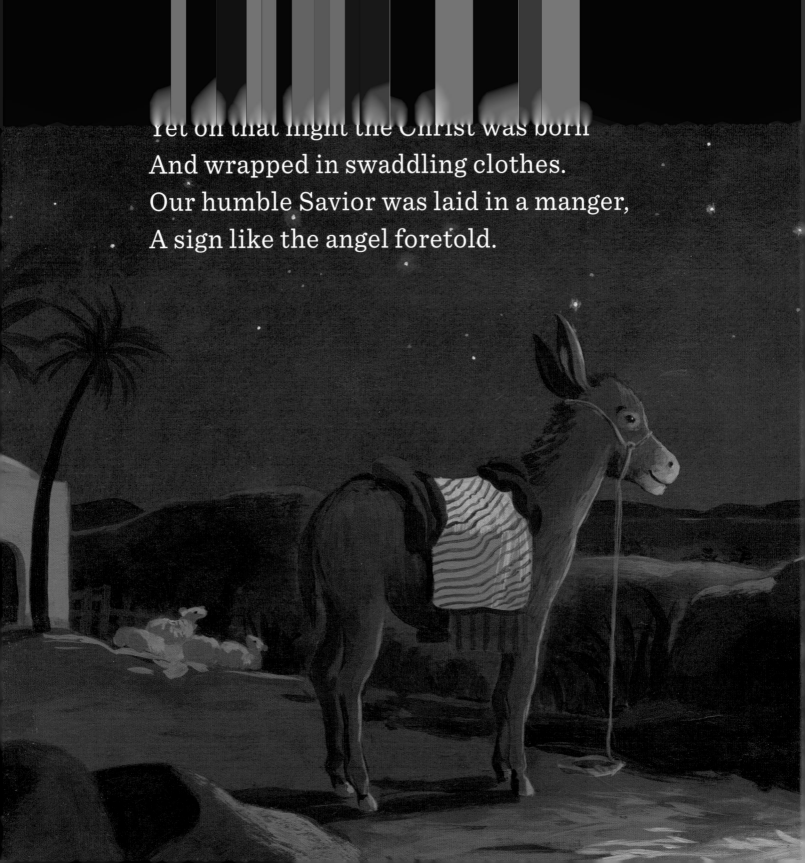

Yet on that night the Christ was born
And wrapped in swaddling clothes.
Our humble Savior was laid in a manger,
A sign like the angel foretold.

The shepherds came; the animals came,
As angel choirs were singing,
Where love came down to make amends
While the world was sleeping.

Glory to God in the highest place!
Hallelujah, our Savior is here!
Merry Christmas to all from heaven to earth,
And to all a happy New Year!